RISING ABOVE

GW00538314

A Guide to Overcoming Life's Challenges.

Vandudzai Mamutse Makhuza

Susan, you have the grace to soar above every challenge!

Makhuza 30/03/19

All Bible quotations are taken from the New King James Version.

ISBN: 978-1-9164022-0-1

Published by Purposeful Platforms by Vandudzai Makhuza

Email: makhuv@hotmail.com

Edited by Effie Kandiwa

Artwork & Photography by John Murinye

DEDICATION

To all the individuals who are thriving to rise above the challenges they are facing in life without throwing in the towel.

TABLE OF CONTENTS

ACKNOWLEDGEMENTS

I am grateful to God for upholding me even when I did not believe in myself. Without His guidance, my life would be meaningless.

I appreciate my parents for nurturing me and instilling in me the confidence that as a girl child I matter. Mum and Dad your encouragement and discipline shaped me to be the woman I am today. I love you Mhamha naBaba!

To my darling Paul, thank you for giving me room to *Rise Above,* it was not easy but by God's grace we are here. I love you Darlie.

To our children, thank you for being yourselves and for checking on my progress since the day you knew I was writing. *Nyasha*, the first fruit of my womb, my pride and joy, I treasure your encouragement and passion sweetie. *Michael Paul*, my loving and caring son, I appreciate your kindness buddy and your openness is like a ray of sunshine. *Hadassah*, my princess, your smile lights up my heart and I treasure every random, warm hug and cuddle we share. Even when I have my head down trying to concentrate I cannot resist your arms wide open and your sweet voice saying, *"mummy hug!"*. I am blessed to be your mother and I am grateful to God for the heritage I have in you.

To my sisters and brother, thank you for turning me towards God, although I do not think you realise that is what you do. In some of you I now have prayer partners and united we are standing focused on God. I love and appreciate you all.

FOREWORD

Truly, we must "never judge a book by its size and cover but by its valuable contents." The real value of any worthy vessel in life is hidden right inside, not outside. Without a shadow of doubt, Vandudzai has injected in this book, great insight for anyone who desires to rise above every negative and sour situation. The style and structure of this book makes it more engaging and inspiring through simple down to heart tips.

It would be an impossible mission to take anyone through a situation the height you have not overcome. The ability to rise above difficulties in life is embedded inside the realisation of our purpose on earth. A man without purpose is bound to failure and hopelessness. That is why every Christian should learn to understand that, **"to everything there is a season, and a time to every purpose under the heaven." Ecclesiastes 3:1**. Passing through any situation in life has its purpose and it would only make sense to understand the purpose for such a season and thereby remain focused to get through the tunnel to see the bright light at the other end. Knowing your purpose in life would aid you through thick and thin no matter what happens.

What makes this book "Rising Above" so unique is its simplicity in presentation, biblical relevancy and reliability. Are you ready to "rise above"? Ultimately, this is the book for you. I personally cherished what the writer says toward the end of this book, "as God reveals His purpose for your life, run with the purpose for His grace is sufficient for you. Grace is the energy we need to fulfil purpose".

With passion, I recommend this book with conviction that it will rebirth your hope and joy in fulfilling God's purpose for your life. As you open the passages of this book, my prayer is that you will be richly blessed in Jesus Mighty Name.

Emmanuel Ilori (RCCG Ireland)

INTRODUCTION

God created us for a purpose and His desire is for every one of us to fulfil that God ordained purpose. As we fellowship closely with God we discover the very reason why He created us. It was through fellowship that God gave Adam responsibility in the garden of Eden (**Genesis 2:15**). I pray we will not fail God by walking out of His plan and purpose for our lives. We can support and help each other in the process of fulfilling purpose but everyone must maximise their potential to achieve.

As we endeavour to succeed in the journey of life the devil is working tirelessly to destroy the very purpose of God in our lives. He is busy trying to pull us down and discourage us in every way possible. He is infiltrating our relationships with one another sowing sour grapes. When we have tasted the grapes of betrayal we lose the desire to fellowship with others, therefore the purpose of

God for human kind is hindered. When God created man, He said be fruitful and multiply. How can we be fruitful without fellowship? The devil is also busy at work trying to distract us from having fellowship with God, if he succeeds in that there is no hope for us of fulfilling purpose until fellowship with God is restored.

We read in the book of Genesis chapter 26 that Isaac was prospering in Gerar and the Philistines envied him, they filled the wells his father Abraham dug with mud and he was sent away by King Abimelech because he was mightier than them. Isaac did not fight back neither did he compromise his ways of doing things so that he could stay but he moved on. When Isaac pitched his tent and dug wells in the valley of Gerar, the herdsmen of Gerar strove with his herdsmen. Each time this happened Isaac would just move on and dig another well until they were not fighting him anymore. From this passage, I learnt that Isaac did not waste his precious time and energy arguing and fighting but that he remained focused and tended to what God had blessed him with. He did not lose sight of his God given purpose because of the challenges he faced. God saw his determination and came to fellowship with him again and renewed the covenant He made with Abraham his father (**Genesis 22:16:18**). When his enemies saw how God prospered him, they came to make peace with him. This reminds me of this scripture, "**When a man's ways please the LORD, He makes even his enemies to be at peace with him." (Proverbs 16:7 New Kings Version)**

Isaac discovered his purpose through fellowship with God and he made up his mind that nothing was going to hinder him from becoming a great nation. He might have been offended when the Philistines filled up the wells dug by his father, but he did not react foolishly. The Philistines tampered with his inheritance from his earthly father, but he considered the inheritance from our

Heavenly Father of greater importance therefore he did not fight with them. Eventually his enemies gave up, they realised they were contending with a greater power and sought peace.

Jesus Christ, our forerunner was born and lived here on earth just like you and me. He had a purpose and His purpose was to save His people from their sins (Matthew 1:21) as revealed by the angel of the Lord to Joseph. The devil proposed in his heart that Jesus would not fulfil purpose and set out to tempt Him, but he was disappointed when Jesus overcame temptation by the word of God. When Jesus came to the river Jordan to be baptised, John publicly pronounced the very reason Jesus was on planet earth; to take away the sin of the world!

"The next day John saw Jesus coming toward him, and said, "Behold! The Lamb of God who takes away the sin of the world!" John 1:29

After Jesus was baptised, He was led by the Holy Spirit into the wilderness to be tempted by the devil. Of course, Jesus had a purpose from God the Father and the Holy Spirit (**The Trinity at work**) led Him to be tempted by the devil (**Matthew 4:1-11**). Jesus overcame the temptations and fulfilled His purpose. If Jesus fell into the temptations, there is no way He would have taken the sin of the world. Falling into temptation would have rendered Him sinful and unworthy to take anyone's sin. The devil made several attempts on Jesus, but He remained steadfast. The same devil who was permitted to tempt Jesus and Job, can still tempt us today as this is part of his mission. As children of The Almighty God, we have been given authority to tread over all the power of the enemy and victory has been promised us. Let us use our authority in Jesus name.

"Behold, I give you the authority to trample on serpents and scorpions, and over all the

power of the enemy, and nothing shall by any means hurt you." Luke 10:19

In the pages of this book I will be highlighting how we can overcome and rise above difficult situations and circumstances we encounter through the word of God. Reference will be made of how some people, who are recorded in the pages of the Bible overcame temptations and difficult situations through their trust and reliability in God. May the Holy Spirit help us to let the Word of God be the weapon of our warfare in Jesus Mighty name. As we fellowship with God we discover our purpose, the very reason why God created us and we are empowered to accomplish that purpose. When we fulfil purpose, God is glorified, and the devil is shamed. Let us endeavour to live our lives for the glory of God. The scriptures I referred to in this book have helped and are still helping me as I strive to Rise Above and endeavour to fulfil purpose. I hope you will be encouraged as well.

CHAPTER ONE

RISING ABOVE FEAR

The Oxford dictionary defines fear as an unpleasant emotion caused by the threat of danger, pain, or harm. Deducing from the above definition and my own personal experience fear is not a positive emotion. Fear takes away instead of edifying, it robs one of joy, peace and hope among other positive emotions. Fear does not improve one's wellbeing, therefore it should not be allowed to linger for long in a person's life, unless one wants to live a defeated life they should not allow fear to dominate them. Events and situations which trigger the emotion of fear are inevitable but what matters is our response to them. Do we allow fear to dominate our whole being and do we approach every situation in life with fear? Fear is unavoidable, but it can be overcome by the grace of God as He assures us in the book of Isaiah;

"Fear not, for I *am* with you,

Be not dismayed, for I *am* your God.

I will strengthen you,

Yes, I will help you,

I will uphold you with My righteous right hand." Isaiah 41:10

When fear strikes, we should immediately remember that God is with us to help us overcome it. We should not allow fear to rule our lives, but we should strive to rise above it as well as other negative emotions. When the devil throws his wicked darts at us through various afflictions triggering fear we should always remember the promise of God that He is with us always to strengthen and help us in moments of fear. Our God knew and still knows that fear is inevitable therefore He made Himself available to help us. No matter what we go through we should not allow discouragement and fear to dominate us, as the result of fear is always defeat.

All negative emotions come from the enemy of our souls, the devil. He feeds on our fear therefore when we live in it, the devil is enabled to produce doubt and hopelessness among other negatives that he has to offer. When faith is activated in us there is no room for fear to grow in turn starving the devil. The devil then leaves us as he cannot stay where he is not being fed. Fear and faith cannot coexist. The devil manipulates us by striking on our weaknesses and struggles. He can also use people around us such as friends, colleagues and family members. In other words, the devil uses whoever he finds to be the weakest link to accomplish his purpose which is to kill, to steal and to destroy as stated in,

"The thief does not come except to steal, and to kill, and to destroy." *John 10:10a*

These people can be used to discourage us through words from their mouths which could be piercing to our hearts. Their words can be discouraging so much that we become weak and hopeless. Fear gives birth to hopelessness and hopelessness gives birth to fear and the cycle continues unless we rise above the fear. May God help us to be alert to the schemes of the evil one that when his agents begin to accuse us, blame us and throw all sorts of evil darts towards us we will have the faith and courage to stand on the promises of God and not be afraid. After telling us why the devil came, Jesus also tells us why He also came:

"I have come that they may have life, and that they may have it more abundantly." John 10:10b

In any area of our lives that the enemy has made us to feel hopeless, discouraged and tormented, Jesus is ready to restore us. Jesus came to give us hope, encouragement and to bring life to every dead situation in our lives. All that we should do is to surrender our all to Him and let Him have His way in our lives. God specialises in restoring those situations which the devil has destroyed and brings light to the dark areas of our lives. Let us allow him to fulfil His purpose in our lives. He is the only one who has promised us victory. In fact, He has already won the victory when He died on the Cross of Calvary, was buried and resurrected on the third day, all we should do is to have faith in Him. He is the only one reliable and available day and night to help us out of every fearful and distressing situation.

Often, when we are afraid we tend to call for help and from the wrong places and wrong people, leaving out the one who said,

"Call unto me and I will answer you and show you great and mighty things, which you do not know." Jeremiah 33:3

God promised to uphold us because He knew that we are weak and easily discouraged. In our discouraged state, we become fearful and unable to stand on our own, that is when we need the Great and Mighty God to help us. It is in these distressing times that we must lift our faith in God for He is our very present help in times of need.

PRAYER POINTS

1.Heavenly father please take away fear from me and give me the boldness and a sound mind to cry out to you when I am afraid. **(2Timothy 1:7)**

2.Have mercy on me dear Lord for those times I did not depend on you and for the times I have made decisions based on my fears instead of faith.

3. Thank you Lord Jesus for coming to give and restore life to me. I thank you, for the life I now live, I live in you. **(Galatians 2:20)**

4. Thank you Lord for shielding me from the arrows which were sent to destroy your purpose in my life. **(Isaiah 54:17)**

AMEN!

Points of Reflection

_____

_____

_____

_____

_____

_____

_____

_____

_____

_____

_____

CHAPTER TWO

OVERCOMING DISTRESS

Let us look at how David responded to a very distressing situation when he and his army returned to Ziklag to find the city burnt down, their wives and children taken captives by the Amalekites. It is important to note that David's two wives were also taken captive (**1 Samuel 30**). On realizing their loss David and his men wept until they were weak and hopeless. Instead of the men gathering strength by encouraging each other to pursue the Amalekites and rescue their families they thought of stoning their leader David who was also in the same predicament as them. In their eyes, their families were beyond reach but they had someone they could blame for their loss. The men ganged up against David and plotted to

stone him to death, on realizing their evil plan
David became greatly distressed, his friends were
now his foes. He encouraged himself in the Lord
God. He knew that he needed God's right hand
to uphold him, therefore he enquired of the Lord
and God replied promptly telling him to pursue
and recover all without fail.

**"So David inquired of the LORD, saying, "Shall
I pursue this troop? Shall I overtake them?"
And He answered him, "Pursue, for you shall
surely overtake *them* and without fail recover
all." 1 Samuel 30:8**

When David got to the camp finding it invaded,
burnt down and families taken captive, he started
counting the loss and wailed like every other man
following him instead of taking a leader's position.
The more they wept the weaker they became. His
men looked up to him for guidance and
leadership, but he was also crying just like any
one of them. No wonder why they wanted to

stone him, he failed to take a leadership position. They felt let down at such a time they needed a leader to encourage them and give them hope. As David and all the man with him were returning to Ziklag, every one of them was very much looking forward to being reunited with his family, unfortunately when they got to their camp the enemy had invaded it, stole from them, burnt the camp down and took their children and wives captive. There was no sign of life at the camp. Hope was taken away and they were all dismayed. The situation became even worse for David as those he was wailing with spoke of stoning him. David became distressed and it was in this moment of distress that David remembered to call on God. Had he continued in that discouraged disposition and distress, I am sure that he would have been stoned to death, fulfilling the purpose of the enemy which is to steal, kill and to destroy. Everyone could have lost because the

Amelekites would have continued to go further from Ziklag.

Glory be to God for David remembered the God of his strength and he was surely strengthened. From this we learn that we should not focus on the calamity, the loss or even the negative reports that we are hearing but we should focus on God. Change of focus does not mean you have already recovered but it simply means that you have faith that God can give you victory over every negative emotion in Jesus name. He can deliver, heal and give you total restoration if you lift faith instead of fear. Beloved, in every situation let us have the mindset to quickly enquire of the next steps from God. When we seek His counsel, He is always faithful to answer and give us assurance of victory. As the head of the family or if you are in any leadership position, please do not make the mistake of crying in defeat just like everybody else you are leading, you are like the commander in chief of the army therefore arise, encourage yourself and enquire of the Lord. Just imagine how chaotic it can be in a family when the father, the mother and the children all cry for food instead of the father to brace himself up and go out to look for bread to feed his family.

When the Amalekites burnt Ziklag, they left it burning to ashes and took the women and children captive. David and his men came back and realised their loss. They cried hopelessly until they put the blame on David and wanted to stone him to death. This threat caused David much stress as he was sure that the vagabonds he had trained and empowered were going to kill him. These men had become his family but at that moment they were plotting against him. We also find that in our lives, most times our distress is not in the hands of strangers but from those close to us whom at times we have gone out of our way to help. The men who were with David lost focus and allowed their intentions to be determined by their emotions. Unfortunately, what they had intended to do, that is stoning David was not going to restore their families nor possessions. Instead of them putting their heads together and coming up with a strategy to go after their enemy they blamed their own leader David, whilst their enemy was going further away. The thought of being stoned must have been heart breaking for David who also had his two wives taken captive. His now extended family held him responsible for their loss and wanted him to pay with his own life. David felt exposed by men but glory to God, he remembered the God in heaven who promised to help and uphold those who call upon Him. There is need for us to confess that we will not rely on any man, but we shall put our trust in God.

"I lift up my eyes to the mountains, where does my help come from? My help comes from the LORD, the Maker of heaven and earth. He will not let your foot slip he who watches over you will not slumber;" Psalm 121:1-3

No matter how weak we are, the Lord has promised to make us a new sharp threshing instrument to destroy the mountains and make hills as chaff that is blown by the wind. (*Isaiah 41:15*) Hallelujah for we serve a God who empowers us.

After David sought the Lord and was given assurance to pursue, overtake and recover all, he now had the confidence to call his army to follow him to go and rescue their families. It was after his communion with God that he was strengthened for victory.

On that note, we should learn and understand that communion with God is beneficial to us in all situations for God knows the end from the beginning. Those who were plotting to stone David were now prepared to go after the Amalekites with him to rescue their families. David knew that with God on his side he was an overcomer. As the head of your family, when calamity strikes your household that is not the time to sit and be hopeless but arise and call upon God for direction. It is always important to remember that fear is not from God as the scriptures say:

"For God has not given us a spirit of fear, but of power and of love and of a sound mind." 2 Timothy 1:7

All the Amalekites who tried to resist David and his men from recovering their wives and children perished by the hand of God for He was the one upholding David. As we arise to recover everything the enemy has robbed us, we will succeed, and the enemy will become as nothing before us in Jesus name. When David focused on the loss he cried in despair, then the situation got even worse when his men became his enemies. At that moment, he turned to God and it pleased God who caused his men to gather with him again. Surely when a man's ways please the

Lord, He makes his enemies to be at peace with him.

"When a man's ways please the LORD, He makes even his enemies to be at peace with him." Proverbs 16:7

PRAYER POINTS

1. Heavenly father I reject the spirit of fear operating in my life in any form or shape. I receive the spirit of boldness and sound mind to walk by faith without being intimidated. **(2 Timothy 1:7)**

2. Heavenly Father help me not to spend much time counting my loss but give me the grace to call upon you as soon as I realize the attack of the enemy in my life.

3. Heavenly Father help me to live a life that is pleasing to you and make my enemies to be at peace with me. **(Proverbs 16:7)**

4. Heavenly Father give me victory over my enemies in Jesus mighty name. **(Psalm 44:7)**

5. Arise oh Lord and let my enemies be scattered. I decree that the Egyptians I see today I will see them no more as they will become as nothing before you my father. **(Exodus 14:13)**   **AMEN!**

Points of Reflection

CHAPTER THREE

THE WILDERNESS EXPERIENCE

Are you in need and living in depression and oppression? The Lord said, He will hear you and never leave you. Please note that for one to be heard they should cry out, if one remains silent they will not be heard. God said that He will open rivers in high places and fountains amid valleys to meet our needs. God made a way for the Israelites through the Red Sea, He provided water for them from the rock. He is the same God who provided water for Hagar to give to Ishmael when he was about to die of thirst in the wilderness. Whatever wilderness experience you are going through call on God, He will hear and deliver you by His right hand of power.

"So Moses brought Israel from the Red Sea; then they went out into the Wilderness of

Shur. And they went three days in the wilderness and found no water." Exodus 15:22

Immediately after the victory of crossing the Red Sea, the children of Israel faced a challenge of walking in the wilderness without water for three days. Eventually they came to the bitter waters of Marah and they could not drink it. The Israelites murmured against Moses their leader, they even wished that if only they had remained in slavery in Egypt. Moses knew too well how to call on God who showed him the remedy for the bitter water. Complaining does not bring about any solution to a problem. The more one complains the more they lose focus and feel hopeless. Unlike David who cried like a common person, Moses chose to call on God for help instead of murmuring against Him. They were only able to drink the water after Moses cried unto God. It is not the bitterness of your situation which is keeping God away from helping you but your own failure to call on Him.

Sometimes we examine our situations and think that they are too difficult for God, we underestimate the power of God when He Himself said that He is the Almighty there is nothing too difficult for Him. We should stop limiting God from doing what He does best which is saving us from all kinds of destruction.

"Behold, I *am* the Lord, the God of all flesh. Is there anything too hard for Me?" Jeremiah 32:27

It does not matter the challenging situation you are facing right now, call on God, He hears and delivers. It is high time we desist from murmuring and blaming leaders and others for our calamities. The more we complain the more we are entangled and drowned into our difficulties without a way out. Murmuring magnifies the bitter situation. Our deliverance is in calling on God not in murmuring or on how long we focus on a bitter situation and get discouraged. Moses could have murmured as well, since he was also thirsty like everyone else, but he knew that the promise of God was to bring them to a land flowing with milk and honey. Hold on to the promise!

"So I have come down to deliver them out of the hand of the Egyptians, and to bring them up from that land to a good and large land, to a land flowing with milk and honey........."
Exodus 3:8

When the Israelites got to the flooded Red Sea and the Egyptians were following behind them, fear came upon them and they murmured but Moses sought God. When they became thirsty and could not drink from the waters of Marah they murmured again but Moses sought God who provided a solution to heal the water. One would think that the Israelites would have learnt their lessons to fully trust in God from miraculously crossing the Red Sea and God healing the waters of Marah but they had not. They were so accustomed to murmuring against God and blaming Moses. They did not take responsibility but made Moses and Aaron responsible for their leaving Egypt as if they were the only two who wanted to be out of slavery. Moses had already run away but God sent him back to lead Israel out of slavery. When they were hungry in the wilderness they thought of the bread of sorrow they ate in Egypt instead of calling on Jehovah Jireh who promised them a land flowing with milk and honey. They were so accustomed to slavery to the extent that whenever they faced a challenge they were not looking ahead but behind and wishing to go back. This is exactly what most of us do, we still envy our bitter past when God is delivering us out of slavery into a better place flowing with milk and honey. Each time we hit a brick wall we give up and turn back instead of gathering strength and scaling up the wall until we go over to the other side or even go along the wall until we find an entrance or reach the end of it.

There is no gain in giving up, so I encourage you to arise and face the challenge by the grace of God.

Moses could have given up on the Israelites because of their murmuring and lack of faith but he kept on calling on God for help. Despite all the challenges they faced on their journey Moses was determined to get to the Promised Land but unfortunately, he could not enter because he angrily reacted to his brethren's murmuring. He became distressed and carried God's instructions in anger, he became a fool by allowing anger to reside in his heart.

"Do not hasten in your spirit to be angry, For anger rests in the bosom of fools." Ecclesiastes 7:9

Fear triggers a whole lot of negative emotions. The children of Israel were afraid to perish of hunger and thirst in the wilderness therefore they complained, Moses got discouraged and became angry. In this case, Moses did not cry out to God for his anger which resulted in him missing out on the promise. Moses was good in praying and interceding for others but not for himself. May God open our eyes to any emotion that could hinder us from making it to eternal life.

Leaders, be alert and have confidence in Christ to the extent that those you are leading will not cause you to sin against God and miss the promised land. Always remember that they are not the ones who have put you in position so do not allow them to stop you from fulfilling purpose. When Moses went up the mountain to meet with God, the children of Israel were afraid thinking that they have been abandoned by Moses and God, therefore they convinced Aaron to mould a golden calf for them to worship instead of worshipping God who delivered them from slavery with a mighty hand. They desired fellowship with idols instead of God. On returning to the camp Moses' anger was rekindled and he broke the tablets of the law. Moses allowed anger to have him, he did not rule over it. We receive grace from God to rule over anger. **(Genesis 4:7b).**

PRAYER POINTS

1. Heavenly father, help me to look up to you during calamity, teach me not to seek security or approval from man. **(Psalm 121:1)**

2. Heavenly Father, help me to have confidence that you can fulfill what you promised. Help me acknowledge the victories you gave me, you did not allow the enemy to outrun me with my possessions.

3. Let my mouth be filled with praises instead of murmuring. Let praises continually flow from my heart in Jesus name. **(Psalm 34:1)**

4. Heavenly Father teach me to view every situation from your perspective instead of man's or my own perspective

5. Heavenly father let my walk with you not be influenced by what I hear or see. **(2 Corinthians 5:7)** Teach me to obey your commands despite my emotions and fears.

AMEN!

Points of Reflection

_____

_____

_____

_____

_____

_____

_____

_____

_____

_____

CHAPTER FOUR

RISING ABOVE REJECTION

Rejection can be defined as failure to show due affection or concern for someone. When one is rejected they are dismissed as inadequate or unacceptable. Rejection triggers all sorts of negative emotions as well and if care is not taken those emotions can lead to negative actions.

In the household of father Abram, strife arose between Sarai and her maidservant Hagar. Sarai could not wait for God's rightful time to fulfill His promise to Abram therefore she gave her maidservant Hagar to her husband as a concubine, the decision Sarah lived to regret after Hagar conceived and despised her. Wait on God to fulfill His promise upon your life and family and do not fall into the temptation of trying to help God!

41

Later, the promised child Isaac was born through Abraham and Sarah. The seed of strife grew and began to manifest between the children and Sarah was displeased and decided to send Hagar and her son Ishmael away. This decision grieved Abraham but God spoke to him to let Hagar and Ishmael go and he obeyed.

"So Abraham rose early in the morning and took bread and a skin of water; and putting *it* on her shoulder, he gave *it* and the boy to Hagar, and sent her away. Then she departed and wandered in the Wilderness of Beersheba." Genesis 21:14

Hagar was given only the supplies which she could carry meaning they were not going to last for a long time. Hagar was rejected by her mistress and by the father of her son. As she wondered in the wilderness with her son, bread and water they had ran out. They were all alone, hungry, thirsty, and they grew weary and hopeless. Hagar could not bear to see her son dying so she left him and sat afar off where she could not see him die.   Out of the pain of abandoning her child in his time of need, Hagar lifted her voice and wept. Ishmael who was unwillingly let go by his father and abandoned by his mother in his moment of weakness cried unto God who hears the cries of his children.

"And God heard the voice of the lad. Then the angel of God called to Hagar out of heaven, and said to her, "What ails you, Hagar? Fear not, for God has heard the voice of the lad where he is." Genesis 21:17

God heard the voice of the lad and called unto his mother and told her not to fear but to arise and act. God heard the desperate cry of Ishmael and delivered him and reaffirmed the promise of him becoming a great nation. Ishmael did not die in the wilderness before becoming a great nation. It does not matter how you have been rejected and abandoned, God sees and hears you when you cry out to Him. When God hears the cry for help, He answers and delivers. May our ears be open to hear God speak and our eyes be open to see the well of water like Hagar. She gave the water to Ishmael and he was revived.

"Arise, lift up the lad and hold him with your hand, for I will make him a great nation."[19] Then God opened her eyes, and she saw a well of water. And she went and filled the skin with water and gave the lad a drink." Genesis 21:18-19

Perhaps you are a mother who has been abandoned and your children neglected by their biological father or you know someone in that situation I would encourage you to put your trust in God. Stop fighting your own battles but cry out to God who is not deaf to hear your cry and His hand is long enough to help you. If Hagar resorted to staying and fight Sarah, I don't think she was going to have the encounter she had with God in the wilderness. Sometimes God takes us out of our comfort zones and brings us into wilderness experiences not to harm us but to take us to a promised land. Hagar made a wise choice to leave Abraham's household with her son when she was told to do so, and God did not send her back like He did when she ran away earlier before giving birth to Ishmael.

Hagar and Ishmael left with nothing out of all of Abraham's possessions. They were not given even a donkey to ride on their journey or to carry their personal belongings. They only left with enough bread and water that Hagar could carry on her shoulder, but God provided for them in the wilderness as Ishmael became a skilled hunter. Why waste time fighting a man over possessions instead of looking unto Jehovah Jireh? When the situation was at its worst Hagar interceded for her son. She took her eyes off seeing her son dying and cried out to God and He answered. Mother, arise and intercede for your children, do not just sit and watch the fruit of your womb wasting away. Make up your mind and say I am not going to sit here and watch my flesh and blood perish.

Have an attitude of the four lepers who decided to go to the camp of the Syrians where there was food instead of dying of hunger as outcasts. When the lepers arose, the whole city had food to eat and were in possession of everything the Syrians left behind when God caused them to flee. As you arise in the place of prayer for your children, the Almighty God will arise to defend and favour your children in Jesus Mighty Name!

"Now there were four leprous men at the entrance of the gate; and they said to one another, "Why are we sitting here until we die? 4 If we say, 'We will enter the city,' the famine *is* in the city, and we shall die there. And if we sit here, we die also. Now therefore, come, let us surrender to the army of the Syrians. If they

keep us alive, we shall live; and if they kill us, we shall only die." ⁵ And they rose at twilight to go to the camp of the Syrians; and when they had come to the outskirts of the Syrian camp, to their surprise no one *was* there." 2 Kings 7:3-5

As we arise in the place of prayer our generation and generations after us will be delivered.

Maybe you have been tricked into having a child or children with a married man and you are now all alone with your children, feeling neglected, abandoned and rejected please stop fighting and resorting to dirty tricks for what does not belong to you. Whether you knew that the man was married or not before you got involved with him, the fact remains he is a married man and now you know that he is married, and you have been tricked! Are you still hurt because you were promised heaven on earth when he sends his wife packing? Now you know better, his wife is not going anywhere because of you therefore move on with your life. Do not waste your time praying and fasting asking God to put them asunder because God will not go against his word, **Mark 10:9 "Therefore what God has joined together, let not man separate."** The man is not your husband, what you have is a child or children with him and that's how far it can go. Therefore, turn your eyes unto the merciful God and lift your voice to intercede for your children.

Choose not to focus on the disappointment and pain but focus on God. Do not fall into the temptation of using children as battle axes neither should you turn the children against their father because whatever has transpired between the two of you has nothing to do with them. Do not let your children carry the burden of how your life turned out, simply because you fell pregnant with them during the season you were deceived. Give your children a break, all they need is to be loved and nurtured. They were not part of your decision making then so why blame them for your bad choices? Stop blaming them and start loving them unconditionally for a change.

Once one parent starts imputing negativity into their children's minds concerning the other parent, be rest assured that you have started breeding bitterness and anger in the children towards their father or mother. When children are angry and embittered against their parents they are no longer honouring their father and mother and you as a parent you are not bringing them up as God commanded.

"'Honour your father and mother," which is the first commandment with promise: [3] "that it may be well with you and you may live long on the earth." [4] And you, fathers, do not provoke your children to wrath, but bring them up in the training and admonition of the Lord." Ephesians 6:2-4

Parents please, do not hinder your children from enjoying the promise of long life from God. When God said, children honour your father and mother, He did not give any exceptions. The honouring is not conditional therefore children must simply honour. If you want to help your children help them to honour God and His word. Well, you may have reasons to justify why you will not allow that man in your children's lives ever again after how he treated you. The truth of the matter is that you are being selfish and denying those children you call yours the blessing of God. So, what good are you doing if you are hindering your children from obtaining God's blessing? Stop being self-centered and if the pain is too deep, ask God to heal you and mend your broken heart. When God gave the command that children should honour their parents He knew that some parents would neglect and abandon their children yet still, He did not give exceptions and conditions that children should only honour those parents who are involved in raising them.

Allow God to heal your broken heart so that you can begin to see clearly. It was only when God spoke to Hagar that her eyes were opened, and she saw a well of water nearby. Some mothers have been badly hurt that they have a possessive hold on their children even when things are bad they can still stand and watch their children suffer. Be like Hagar who said I will not hold on to my son until he dies therefore she lay him down and walked away in total surrender. Hagar said I have done what I could possibly do but now my water and bread is finished, and my son Ishmael is about to die therefore take over Lord. Abraham did not let Ishmael go because he did not love him, it grieved him to let his son go but God told Abraham to listen to his wife Sarah

"And the matter was very displeasing in Abraham's sight because of his son.[12] But

God said to Abraham, "Do not let it be displeasing in your sight because of the lad or because of your bondwoman. Whatever Sarah has said to you, listen to her voice; for in Isaac your seed shall be called. [13] Yet I will also make a nation of the son of the bondwoman, because he *is* your seed." Gen 21:11-13

God told Abraham that He will make a nation out of Ishmael. When faced with a difficult situation Abraham was grieved and God spoke but note that when God spoke to him He did not speak a way out or say Ishmael should remain, but He promised to be with him wherever he went. Therefore, Abraham had to let go of his seed. When Hagar and Ishmael were wandering in the wilderness of Beersheba, Hagar could only feed her son from Abraham's provisions she had carried but those provisions soon ran out. She could not help her child anymore, so she left him. By leaving him she accepted that she was inadequate and in need of help therefore she lifted her voice and wept for her child and the God who hears wilderness cries heard her and answered.

When Hagar cried, God heard Ishmael's voice, so mothers arise and intercede for your children. When she cried out, the very present help in times of need heard her and empowered her.

"God *is* our refuge and strength,
A very present help in trouble." Psalm 46:1

God commanded her to arise and lift Ishmael up and to hold him in her hand for God was making him a great nation. Women let us arise in a place of prayer and hold our children. Despite our weariness and pain let us arise in the place of intercession. If we do not pray for the fruits of our wombs no one else will do it for them. Hagar could have been thirsty and even more hungry than Ishmael, but I do not think that she ate the last piece of bread nor drank the last drop of water. But glory to God she still managed to let out a loud cry unto the Lord. God used Hagar to lift Ishmael from dying of thirst and He also wants to use us to fulfill His plan for our children. Are we willing to be used by God? Or when God says, "Arise!" are we saying,

"But Lord how can I …?" Instead of just doing what we are told. It is not until we arise that God will open our eyes to greatness. Are we going to remain silent and perish with our children?

Some parents are holding back the destinies of their children by harboring anger and bitterness. Release your children and let God have His way in their lives. He wants to use you to help your children stand but not until you let go of them first. For example, Moses before the burning bush had to let go of the rod which was in his hand before it could be used for miracles. Surrendering to God brings about transformation!

"So the LORD said to him, "What is that in your hand?" He said, "A rod." And He said,

"Cast it on the ground." So he cast it on the ground, and it became a serpent; and Moses fled from it. Then the LORD said to Moses, "Reach out your hand and take it by the tail" (and he reached out his hand and caught it, and it became a rod in his hand)," Exodus 4:2-4

Rejection may have left your children broken and battered. You have tried your best to raise them single handedly as they say but you cannot do it anymore. Please do not hesitate to surrender them to God. Stand afar off and cry out for help and the Helper will hear you and direct you on how to help your children. He will open your eyes to His provisions. God wants to use you to lift your young and weak children, to hold them and assure them that they can make it despite their situation. Lift them by encouraging, speaking life and hope into them and most importantly teaching them the way of the Lord. Greatness lies in the lives of our children therefore we cannot afford to be careless with them. If we do not know what to do or how to arise in the place of prayer for our children, let us go before God Almighty and ask for help for He is more than able to help us arise. We cannot afford to sleep when the lives and destinies of our children are at stake. Arise in your prayer life and intercede for your children!

For us to fulfill purpose sometimes God strips us of all the comforts and self-reliance. He takes us to a place where we can only but cry out for help. It was only when Hagar was sent away from Abraham's household that she felt helpless and cried out. When she was still in the camp she was a fighter since the day she conceived Ishmael.

"So he went in to Hagar, and she conceived. And when she saw that she had conceived, her mistress became despised in her eyes.[5] Then Sarai said to Abram, "My wrong *be* upon you! I gave my maid into your embrace; and when she saw that she had

conceived, I became despised in her eyes. The Lord judge between you and me."[6] So Abram said to Sarai, "Indeed your maid *is* in your hand; do to her as you please." And when Sarai dealt harshly with her, she fled from her presence.[7] Now the Angel of the Lord found her by a spring of water in the wilderness, by the spring on the way to Shur. [8] And He said, "Hagar, Sarai's maid, where have you come from, and where are you going?" She said, "I am fleeing from the presence of my mistress Sarai." [9] The Angel of the Lord said to her, "Return to your mistress, and submit yourself under her hand." Genesis 16:4-9

The Bible records that since the time she conceived Hagar despised her mistress therefore there was always contention. I want believe Ishmael picked up on that, leading to the incident which caused them to be sent away. Earlier, when Sarai dealt with her harshly, Hagar decided to run away. She did not take responsibility nor humble herself to apologise and submit to her mistress.

Hagar was sent back to Sarai not because God had not seen her affliction but because it was not yet time for the plan and purpose of God concerning Ishmael. In her moment of despair, Hagar called on the name of God. Whom do we call on when we are in despair? Instead of sitting and murmuring against fellow humans and blaming God for your desperate situation, call on the name of the Lord who hears and sees.

"Then she called the name of the Lord who spoke to her, You-Are-the-God-Who-Sees; for she said, "Have I also here seen Him who sees me?" Genesis 16:13

It is left to us to totally obey God's commands. I don't think Hagar obeyed God totally when she was told to go back and submit to Sarah. If she was submissive, how did her son get the boldness to mock Isaac? Children are like sponges, they can easily pick on the relational and situational vibes and begin to act out what they see and hear from their parents or guardians. It is possible that Ishmael heard his mother mocking and criticizing Isaac and he was bold to repeat what he heard. Hagar sowed a seed of rivalry in her son therefore they were cast out. What kind of seeds are we sowing in the lives of our children or those we are raising up?

Another point to note is that you cannot be submitting to someone and be bitter towards them at the same time. Whatever has caused you to be bitter in any relationship, please deal with it before ruining the whole generation. Bitterness gives birth to hatred and in some cases like the case of Ishmael and Isaac they were separated even though both were Abraham's seeds. Glory to God for He had a blessing for Ishmael as well, if not, he could have remained with nothing or even ended up a slave like his mother.

Prayer Points

1. Father help me to cry out to you amid dark situations. Teach me oh Lord to lift my eyes unto you instead of focusing on the difficult situation. **(Psalm 121:1-3)**

2. Heavenly Father help me to remember that you are Jehovah Jireh my Provider whenever I am in need. **(Genesis 22:14)**

3. Lord give me the willpower to stop fighting and leave the battle into your hands for you see my afflictions. **(2 Chronicles 20:15)**

4. Oh Lord teach me to raise my voice to you instead of using my voice to complain and magnify the situation.

5. Heavenly Father have mercy on me in any way in which I have used my children to fight their father/mother.

6. Father bring reconciliation to every relationship I have destroyed. Heal my children and reconcile them back to their father/mother oh Lord. **(Malachi 4:6)**

7. Heavenly Father have mercy on me for I have caused my children to sin against you by not honouring their father and/or mother by the words I have spoken to them and by my actions. **(Ephesians 6:2 and Matthew 18:6)**

8. Heavenly Father uproot every seed of rivalry I may have sown in my children.

9. Jehovah Jireh please open my eyes to your provisions even in the wilderness.

10. Heavenly Father help me to let go of anything that I have acquired by myself just as Abraham let go of Ishmael whom he acquired outside your promise.

11. Help me to arise and intercede for my children in Jesus Mighty Name.

12. Heavenly Father help me to release my children for your use in Jesus name.

13. Father strip me of anything making me comfortable and not cry out to you.

14. Help me to submit wholly to you and to my husband and to authority as you have commanded.

AMEN!

Points of Reflection

_____

_____

_____

_____

_____

_____

_____

_____

_____

_____

CHAPTER FIVE

THERE IS HOPE

You may have been rejected as a child by either of your parents through no fault of your own and you have so many questions in your mind like, "was there something wrong with me that I was rejected or was I/ am I not good enough to be loved and accepted by my parents?". Or it could be that you were made to believe that it was your fault that your parent ended up parenting alone or in a polygamous relationship. All these thoughts have been weighing on you for a long time, today I want you to know that you have a Father who will never leave no forsake you as He said in His word.

"Behold, I *am* with you and will keep you wherever you go and will bring you back to

this land; for I will not leave you until I have done what I have spoken to you." Genesis 28:15

Every God's blessing upon your life will be fulfilled in Jesus name! Maybe you consider your situation desperate and so bad that you have been forgotten and written off, take courage today and cry out to God and He will hear you and begin to relate with you as He did for David. The worst you can do for yourself is to write yourself off therefore if there is still breath in you, take heart and have hope that God will arise for you.

In **1 Samuel 16**, King Saul sinned against God and the kingdom of Israel was taken away from him, it was time for a new king to be anointed. Therefore, God sent Prophet Samuel to Jesse who was David's father to anoint a king from one of his sons. When Jesse and his other sons were sanctified, David was not amongst them. At that moment, even the prophet did not perceive that one of Jesse's sons was not amongst them, but God knew. So, do not lose heart your time shall soon come, just stay where you are until you are called. When you are called to gather with your family go and gather with them even if they gathered before without you. Do not miss your appointed time because of offence.

Jesse made all his sons pass before Prophet Samuel for one of them to be anointed the next king of Israel but amongst those present and sanctified the chosen one, David was not amongst them. God did not allow Samuel to anoint any of the sons present. Prophet Samuel then asked if those who were present were the only sons of Jesse. It was then that he was told that another son, David was herding sheep. Samuel sent for David and there was nothing to be done until he arrived. Take heart, if any of your parents has forgotten you or even your relatives and neighbors do not mention you, when it is time for God to lift you up they will all wait for you.

David was invited to the sacrifice by God when his father had left him out. David the forgotten was anointed to become a giant killer and king of Israel. You will be restored in Jesus Mighty Name!

PRAYER POINTS

1. Heavenly Father, give me the grace to forgive everyone who has rejected me

2. Father heal every wound inflicted upon my heart because of rejection. You are Jehovah Rapha my Healer. **(Exodus 15:26)**

3. Help me to know that my life and calling are in your hands even if my father does not count me in.

4. Father help me to stand to your calling when it is my appointed time. Help me not to listen to criticism which is the weapon the devil uses to pull me down

5. Heavenly father, please help me not to miss my blessing because of offence. When you have lifted me up help me to

remain humble and not to begrudge anyone who rejected, forgotten and despised me.

AMEN!

Points of Reflection

_____

_____

_____

_____

_____

_____

_____

_____

_____

_____

_____

_____

_____

CHAPTER SIX

HOLD ON TO YOUR DREAMS

Despite the challenges and difficulties we face, we should not neglect our dreams. Let us hold on to our dreams despite all the forces working against us. Joseph, the son of Jacob is a good example of one who held on to his dreams. He was a beloved son to his father but hated and rejected by his brothers to the extent of being sold into slavery, Joseph was not separated from his dream. His dream remained with him into slavery and even in the prison. After being betrayed and sold by his brothers Joseph remained faithful to God. God prospered everything Joseph put his hands on and he was promoted as a slave to work in Potiphar's house. When he was going about his duties in Potiphar's household the devil plotted to kill his dream, but Joseph held on to his dream by refusing to sleep with Potiphar's wife. He knew that for his dream to be fulfilled he could not entangle himself with sin. He knew that his dreams were greater than a moment of sinful pleasure with Potiphar's wife. His brothers hated him because he was loved by their father. They sold him into slavery and the Ishmaelites who bought him passed him to Potiphar for sale like a commodity.

Rarely are people rejected by strangers but by those close to their hearts like family members. Joseph was rejected by his own brothers when he brought food to them even though he knew they hated him. He did not bear any grudge against them therefore he obeyed his father when he was sent. He didn't allow bitterness to influence his actions. Had it been that he was bitter he could have turned back when he did not find them where he thought they were but he enquired and kept on searching until he found them. Joseph knew that his brothers hated him for telling their father all the evil they did and because their father loved him most.

"But when his brothers saw that their father loved him more than all his brothers, they hated him and could not speak peaceably to him. [5] Now Joseph had a dream, and he told *it* to his brothers; and they hated him even more." Genesis 37:4-5

They even hated him more when he told them his dreams. Only if they knew they were going to be beneficiaries of his greatness maybe they could have related with him differently. Joseph's dreams were beyond his brothers, that is why he did not abandon his dreams or his faith in God when they sold him. His dreams were also beyond a moment of sinful sexual pleasure with Potiphar's wife. If Joseph had fallen into the snare that could have been the end of him and his dreams like Samson who could not resist Delilah. Sinning with Potiphar's wife once was what the devil wanted to kill Joseph's dream. Do not allow that moment of pleasure to hinder your dreams!

As the Bible mentions that Joseph's brothers hated him and spoke to him harshly and he was quite aware of their hatred but his countenance towards them was not changed. He still obeyed when his father sent him to bring them food. When they sold him, he did not become bitter with them or with God for not stopping them from doing such evil. Even in slavery and in prison he kept praying and following the precepts of God Almighty. He did not allow his circumstances to change his faith nor trust in God. For so many of us when calamity strikes we quickly get angry and grow bitter and start treating our oppressors badly or we go to the extent of blaming God for forsaking us. We begin to justify ourselves and count all the good we have done, thus becoming self-righteous. In the case of Joseph, he could have said that he did well for his brothers despite their hatred. He worked hard and faithfully in Potiphar's household and his master's wife paid him by falsely accusing him. He could have asked why God had allowed all this to befall him. The thought and narration of his ordeal could have driven him away from God. It was not that Joseph was not hurt and or disappointed by what happened to him, but he did not allow other people's actions to determine his future. He held on to God who fulfils promises. He knew his dreams were bigger and God was making a way for him to greatness although it did not seem like so at that moment.

Please do not allow other people's actions against you to rob you of your destiny or whatever they say against you should not become your identity. Avoid dwelling on the negative but keep yourself busy and meditating on the promises of God. Do not allow your mind to be the devil's workshop by being idle. A lot can happen in a workshop depending on who is in charge. If the devil oversees your mind he breeds all kinds of evil and bitterness. Instead get busy in whatever you are assigned to do by God. Joseph did not refuse to run errands for his father even though he knew that his brothers hated him. When they sold him, they thought they were getting rid of him not knowing that they were pushing him towards his dream and putting him in the path of greatness. They didn't know that eventually they would bow down before him fulfilling his dream. They did not feel compassion for their brother when he came out of the pit terrified, but they went on to sell him to strangers. Joseph did not revenge when he had the opportunity to do so when his brothers came to buy grain. At that time, he could have said it is now pay back time so no grain for you despite your desperation. He knew that what they meant for evil God meant it for good. He chose not to be in the place of God to revenge. He chose to forgive his brothers. Forgiveness brings about reconciliation, reunion and unity. Choose to forgive those who have wronged you. It is not in anybody's power to revenge but God's!

"Beloved, do not avenge yourselves, but rather give place to wrath; for it is written, "Vengeance is Mine, I will repay," says the Lord." Romans 12:19

PRAYER POINTS

1. Heavenly Father, please help me to hold on to my dreams even if I am hated for them.

2. Heavenly Father, give me the grace not to lose faith during calamity.

3. Heavenly Father, help me to trust you in the good and bad situations

4. Dear Lord, please help me to remain focused on my dreams and purpose like Joseph who did not fall for just a moment of pleasure, he was focused. **(Philippians 3:14)**

AMEN!

Points of Reflection

_____

_____

_____

_____

_____

_____

_____

_____

_____

_____

_____

<u>CHAPTER SEVEN</u>

WHEN GOD INTERUPTS YOUR PLAN FOR HIS PURPOSE

When Joseph learnt that his fiancée was pregnant before they were married and known each other he decided to separate from Mary but being a just man, he did not want her to be dealt with harshly. As it was communal law then that if an unmarried woman is found to be pregnant she must be cast out of the city and stoned, therefore, Joseph resolved to send Mary away secretly. As he slept pondering on those thoughts, God spoke to him in a dream to take Mary for a wife.

"Now the birth of Jesus Christ was as follows: After His mother Mary was betrothed to Joseph, before they came together, she was found with child of the Holy Spirit. [19] Then

Joseph her husband, being a just *man,* and not wanting to make her a public example, was minded to put her away secretly. 20 But while he thought about these things, behold, an angel of the Lord appeared to him in a dream, saying, "Joseph, son of David, do not be afraid to take to you Mary your wife, for that which is conceived in her is of the Holy Spirit. 21 And she will bring forth a Son, and you shall call His name Jesus, for He will save His people from their sins." 22 So all this was done that it might be fulfilled which was spoken by the Lord through the prophet, saying: 23 "Behold, the virgin shall be with child, and bear a Son, and they shall call His name Immanuel," which is translated, "God with us." 24 Then Joseph, being aroused from sleep, did as the angel of the Lord commanded him and took to him his wife, 25 and did not know her till she had brought

forth her firstborn Son. And he called His name Jesus." Matthew 1:18-25 [18]

I think that when Mary told Joseph about the visit from the angel Gabriel, Joseph did not believe her hence he thought of sending her away. He pondered on how he was going to marry someone who was already pregnant. As he was thinking on how to send Mary away secretly to safety, God knew that the safe place for Mary was in Joseph's house. An angel of the Lord appeared to Joseph in a dream and told him not to be afraid to take his wife Mary as she was conceived of the Holy Spirit and not out of promiscuity. In the dream, God revealed that Mary was to give birth to a Son, they were to name him Jesus and that His purpose was to save people from their sins.

God spoke to Mary and Joseph individually telling them of the greatness they were going to bring up. Their encounters with the angel of God were in private but what they received was too great to remain a private matter. They both resolved as individuals to obey God to fulfill purpose. After hearing from God, they went ahead and got married but Joseph did not know his wife. I think the reason they did that was that they did not want to contaminate the seed of the Holy Spirit. Joseph and Mary protected what God had entrusted to them. They did not allow their fleshly desires to stand in the way of God's purpose. They understood the greatness of what God entrusted upon them.

God has entrusted each one of us with a seed of purpose that we should fulfill. As a seed, it needs to be looked after, watered, the ground around it tilled then as the seed transforms into a plant, it needs to be protected. Once the seed we are carrying has been revealed to us we must make up our minds to cooperate with God and nurture what He has entrusted in us. We should not allow our own fleshly desires to hinder the plan and purpose of God. It must have been so devastating for both Joseph and Mary to hear that she was pregnant until the angel explained the plan and purpose of God.

Mary and Joseph had their own plans, but God had a greater plan for them and they aligned their plan to God's plan. They even changed their wedding day in accordance to the plan of God. We have our plans but are we willing to align our plans to the ultimate plan of God? God knows everything about us, nothing about us is a secret to God and He knows exactly what He can entrust on us in as much as He knew that Joseph was a just man who wouldn't make Mary a public spectacle. Had Joseph been some unjust man, the moment Mary confided in him of her encounter with the angel he could have climbed on the roof top and announced it, leading to Mary being cast out and stoned to death, together with the Hope of salvation. But God chose His candidates wisely among all the engaged couples because He is a wise God. When God looked at

Joseph's heart and thoughts He revealed to him what Mary was carrying. Despite being a just man, Joseph saw it unfit to take Mary as his wife until God sent an angel to him. After the angelic encounter, Joseph took his wife and preserved the seed of salvation to mankind.

As husband or wife can God reveal what He has entrusted into your spouse and trust you to nurture and protect it until purpose is fulfilled? As a parent, can God reveal the stars entrusted upon your children? My beloved, can God work with you? Are we willing to align our plans to God's purpose? From today onwards do not look at your spouse and children ordinarily instead ask God for the grace to see them as God sees them. And when you see them as God sees them cooperate with God for His purpose to be fulfilled in their lives. For husbands and fathers please protect what God has entrusted to you in your wife and your children. They need your covering just as Joseph protected Mary from being stoned to death. Desist from making public the issues that pertain to your household. Joseph and Mary did not go about telling people what was happening in their home or seeking human advice. They could have been advised out of the plan and purpose of God.

If there be anything which has brought you disappointment this season may God appear to you and reveal His purpose in your disappointment and give you counsel. When you receive God's counsel, do as He direct you. Joseph obeyed to take Mary his wife therefore became the earthly father of Jesus Christ, a father who would protect Him among other things involved in raising a child.

When Jesus was born, Herod plotted to kill Him, God appeared to Joseph in a dream again and told him to take Jesus and Mary to safety and they left Bethlehem by night.

"Now when they had departed, behold, an angel of the Lord appeared to Joseph in a dream, saying, "Arise, take the young Child and His mother, flee to Egypt, and stay there until I bring you word; for Herod will seek the young Child to destroy Him." [14] When he arose, he took the young Child and His mother by night and departed for Egypt," Matthew 2:13-14

Joseph was so confident in the word of God that when God spoke Joseph did not need to verify but followed through the word of God. Herod wanted to kill Jesus before fulfilling His purpose, but Joseph was available to take Him to safety. When he was warned that Herod sought to kill Jesus, Joseph did not wait any longer in Bethlehem neither did he go about bidding people farewell, but he left under the cover of the night. There are times we expose ourselves to the enemy by the way we conduct our affairs. Destinies have been robbed and destroyed because of carelessness.

God only allowed the children of Israel to ask from the Egyptians, articles of silver, articles of gold and clothing before they left a place of bondage **(Exodus 12:35-36).** For Joseph, he was to flee in the cover of the night.

The destiny destroyer is always on the look out to snatch away the seed or to destroy your children before they fulfill purpose but as a parent arise and take your children to safety through prayer. God has entrusted them and their destinies into your care and He is more than able to guide you through when you are nurturing them. Have your spiritual antenna tuned to hear God when He speaks. Be ready to take God's instructions no matter how inconvenient they may be. I don't think for a moment that it was easy for Mary and Joseph travelling through the night in unfamiliar territories, but they obeyed God.

God uses the same principle today when giving us purpose and His plan is not to harm us but to bring us to an expected end.

"For I know the thoughts that I think toward you, says the Lord, thoughts of peace and not of evil, to give you a future and a hope." Jeremiah 29:11

When God entrusts and reveals His plan and purpose to us we must yield to Him knowing that He will watch over His word to perform it

"Then the Lord said to me, 'You have seen well, for I am ready to perform My word.'" Jeremiah1:12

It was not a secret to Joseph and Mary who Jesus was as they were told when He was conceived that He was the Savior of God's people but there is nowhere I have read of them bragging and boasting about that. Even when the wise men came to worship Him they remained humble. The key point here is, no matter the greatness of your conception and delivery you should remain humble. Our gifts and achievements should speak for themselves not us proclaiming them from roof tops.

When God gives a blessing, He makes a way and He is with us until the blessing is mature and perfected. The blessing can be given as a seed which needs nurturing to maturity. At times in the process of nurturing the seed, one may need some encouragement and assurance. In the case of Mary, God spoke to her through the angel at conception and when she visited Elizabeth there was confirmation of the word of God. The salutation Mary received from Elizabeth was in line with the word of God from the angel and she was encouraged and praised God.

"And it happened, when Elizabeth heard the greeting of Mary, that the babe leaped in her womb; and Elizabeth was filled with the Holy Spirit. [42] Then she spoke out with a loud voice

and said, 'Blessed *are* you among women, and blessed *is* the fruit of your womb! ......' ⁵⁶ And Mary remained with her about three months and, returned to her house." Luke 1:41-42; 56

After her encounter with the angel of God, Mary did not run to meet the dream killers or her mates, but she ran to Elizabeth whom the angel had revealed to her. When she met Elizabeth, her countenance was lifted, and she magnified the Lord who had remembered her and His people Israel. I highly recommend spending time with people who cause you to magnify God than spending time with those whose outlook to every situation and circumstance is gloom and doom.

Whom we share our visions and accomplishments with really matter. The visions need to be nurtured for them to become a reality and accomplishments need to be maintained and protected. We should be wise in choosing those we share an audience with. Mary did not run to her mates with the revelation of her conception. She could not afford to be careless with what she had just received, therefore she preserved her encounter and when she got to Elizabeth's it was not Mary who spoke first, but Elizabeth confirmed what the angel had said to Mary. If she shared her conception with just about anybody that could have been the end of it as she was going to be ridiculed for falling pregnant before getting married. The news of her pregnancy could have spread like wild fire and she could have been stoned before even Joseph contemplated to send her away secretly. With Elizabeth, Mary was encouraged, and the seed of greatness was preserved and nurtured.

Mary stayed with Elizabeth for three months. It is said that the first three months of pregnancy are crucial. This is the time a woman's body adjusts to accommodate the growing baby at the same time the hormones will be raging affecting emotions and anything at all that can be affected.

It is during this time when a woman needs all the support and encouragement she could possibly get. Mary decided to be at ease in Elizabeth's presence. I want to believe that by the time she went back to her own home she was empowered to stand against any doubt in her mind that she was carrying the Savior of Israel. Her raging hormones had settled. There are times it is very crucial to withdraw from business as usual and focus on the matter at hand without distractions. Associate and spend time with those of the same mind as you and they will encourage you to fulfil the purpose of God, nurturing the seed of greatness in you and not those who will destroy your vision.

It is very important to evaluate how and with whom we are spending our most valuable time. Is there any value being added to us or there is taking away from us? Healthy relationships are meant to edify not to discourage therefore evaluate every relationship and friendship and decide to take a bold step and end unhealthy associations. There are some people who can suck life and energy out of you if you hang around them. Some have the potential to abort what we have conceived of the Holy Spirit and destroy our dreams and visions. Absolutely nothing is worth losing your dreams and visions or aborting your seed for. God has a plan and purpose with very dream and seed He gives His children. At an appropriate time, the visions and dreams will become a reality and the seed will germinate and grow. Even if your dream, vision and seed is unheard of, do not give it up, that is how God works. Noah built an ark, an act that was unheard of, but by faith Noah believed God and obeyed and those who laughed at him perished in the flood, but Noah and his family lived. Joseph's brothers laughed at him when he shared his dream but they laughter did not stop them from eventually bowing down to him when his dream became a reality. Not only did they bow to him

once but several times when the dream became
a reality

PRAYER POINTS

1. Heavenly Father, I ask for grace to hear and obey you when you speak to me.

2. Dear Lord, please help me to protect and nurture those you have entrusted in my care.

3. I receive sufficient grace not to allow my fleshly desires hinder the plan and purpose of God in my life and in the lives of others. **(1 Corinthians 9:27)**

4. Lord, help me to yield and align myself with your ultimate plan for my life in Jesus name.

5. Father, I ask for grace to be humble especially when you reveal your seed of greatness within me.

6. Lord, I ask for grace not to compromise the safety of my spouse and my children.

7. Help me to believe that your purpose and plan for my life is for my good. **(Jeremiah 29:11)**

8. Please give me wisdom **(James 1:5)** to choose the company I keep wisely. **(Psalm 1)**

9. Dear Lord, please give me the courage and boldness to separate/walk away from unhealthy company. **(2 Corinthians 6:14)**

10. Thank you, Father God, for creating me with a purpose. **(Genesis 1:26, Jeremiah 1:5)**

AMEN!

Points of Reflection

CHAPTER EIGHT

YIELDING TO GOD'S CALL

Most times we hold back from fulfilling God's purpose because we seek majority consensus forgetting that when God spoke, He spoke to us as individuals not as a crowd. When Jesus appeared to Saul on the road to Damascus there were other people with him, but the message was directed to him alone.

"**As he journeyed he came near Damascus, and suddenly a light shone around him from heaven. [4] Then he fell to the ground, and heard a voice saying to him, "Saul, Saul, why are you persecuting Me?" [5] And he said, "Who are You, Lord?" Then the Lord said, "I am Jesus, whom you are persecuting. It *is* hard for you to kick against the goads." [6] So he, trembling**

and astonished, said, "Lord, what do You want me to do?" Then the Lord *said* to him, "Arise and go into the city, and you will be told what you must do." [7] And the men who journeyed with him stood speechless, hearing a voice but seeing no one." Acts 9:3-7

Saul later known as Paul was on a mission of his own, but God had a great purpose for him. Saul had his plan on how to execute his mission of persecuting the followers of Christ. He sought permits to go and arrest followers of Christ in Damascus and he also had his own followers helping him in his evil mission.

"Then Saul, still breathing threats and murder against the disciples of the Lord, went to the high priest [2] and asked letters from him to the synagogues of Damascus, so that if he found any who were of the Way, whether men or women, he might bring them bound to Jerusalem." Acts 9:1-2

Saul was very zealous against the Lord's followers and in his mind, he thought he was in charge as he was a symbol of terror to the followers of Christ, but God arose for His own people and He changed Saul's mission. Saul worked tirelessly against the kingdom of God, but God had a plan for him to work tirelessly for His kingdom.

"But the Lord said to him, 'Go, for he is a chosen vessel of Mine to bear My name before Gentiles, kings, and the children of Israel.'" Acts 9:15

Not knowing what lay ahead for him Saul and his team set out for Damascus. When the Lord Jesus appeared to Saul on the way to Damascus, there are some lessons I learnt by the grace of God. When the light from heaven shone around Saul, he realized that he was surrounded by the supernatural power of God and he fell on his knees in surrender and submission to the Lord

Almighty. At that moment the permits he had from the high priest did not matter, for the Chief Priest, the One with the final say had appeared. The authority of Christ is ultimate in every situation! The devil only has power before Christ arises in His power and authority. As Saul fell in submission he heard a voice addressing him by name even though there were others with him. The encounter was for Saul although those who were with him were also transformed by what they witnessed. I did not read anywhere where it says they continued with the mission to persecute followers of Christ, instead they led Saul to where Christ had instructed. In his stubbornness of terrorizing followers of Christ, Saul knew too well that Christ was strong and mighty hence he addressed Him as Lord.

Jesus introduced himself to Saul as the one whom he was persecuting when he was against or after God's followers. Those of us who follow Christ are the apple of His eye. He feels our pain when we are mistreated and He arises to defend us.

"For thus says the Lord of hosts: 'He sent Me after glory, to the nations which plunder you; for he who touches you touches the apple of His eye.'" Zachariah 2:8

The moment Jesus revealed himself to Saul a lot of things changed. Saul asked Him for an assignment, a new direction. In other words, he surrendered to the authority of Christ. When he asked Jesus what He wanted him to do, Saul was further submitting to the Lord's authority as one only takes instructions and assignments from those who have authority over them. It is also possible that Saul realised the magnitude of his actions and considered himself unworthy to have an encounter with Jesus. The Lord Jesus did not appear to Saul to pronounce judgement against him but to give him a new vision and to reveal his purpose. Saul did not bother to justify his actions by answering why he was persecuting Jesus, he just surrendered to the ultimate power. Saul knew that his time was up as the Prince of peace appeared to him. Just at that instant his loyalty changed the devil to Jesus Christ who gave him a new assignment. I can only imagine the joy that was in heaven at Saul's repentance.

"I say to you that likewise there will be more joy in heaven over one sinner who repents than over ninety-nine just persons who need no repentance." Luke 15:7

Jesus did not divert Saul's mission, but He cancelled it. If the mission was diverted he would have finally reached Damascus to persecute the followers of Christ but he arrived with a totally different mission and a new name, Paul. When Saul set out for Damascus he was a symbol of terror to the believers, but he arrived a blind and helpless man depending on others. His identity had been changed.

It is time to examine yourself, in your busy schedule are you busy for God or for yourself? The enemy can keep you occupied outside of God's purpose for your life. Today incline your ear to hear what God is saying to you. What you are doing may be popular but are you sure you are not persecuting Christ? Do not be conscious of yourself and the opinions of those around you, as God's purpose for your life is what matters most right now.

PRAYER POINTS

1.Heavenly Father, have mercy on me and forgive me in any area I have persecuted you

2. Lord I ask for forgiveness in any area that I am not yielding to your call. Today I ask for grace to pay attention to you when you speak.

3. Oh Lord give me the grace not be distracted by the affairs of the world.

AMEN!

Points of Reflection

CONCLUSION

Now that we have an idea of how to use the Word of God in confronting the challenges we face, may God breath strength upon us to rise and fight well, knowing that with Jesus on our side we are fighting from a victorious position.

If you have read through the pages of this book and resolved to "Rise Above" every challenging situation with Jesus, having examined yourself and realised that you have no meaningful fellowship with God, do not wait any longer. Surrender your life to Jesus, repent of all known and unknown sin in your life and ask God to cleanse you by the blood of Jesus. You can now have meaningful fellowship with God. As our relationship with Him is established He guides us through every step as we "Rise Above" situations to fulfil purpose. How wonderful it is to be guided by the one who is victorious. We were created to be above not beneath in Jesus name!

"And the LORD will make you the head and not the tail; you shall be above only, and not be beneath, if you heed the commandments of the LORD your God, which I command you today, and are careful to observe them." Deuteronomy 28:13

THE MAKING OF RISING ABOVE

The inspiration to write this book was given to me several years ago and when it came, the title was very clear. The reason why I did not run with it was because I did not believe in my ability to deliver therefore I started talking myself down. I even questioned the source of the inspiration. I asked myself questions like, of all the people who am I to write a book and even if I write one, who will bother to read it? I lacked self-confidence. The devil had stolen that from me but by the grace of God I am recovering all. Now I know that I can do all things through Christ who strengthens me. **(Philippians 4:13)** I shall fulfil purpose.

I am glad today that in the days of my unbelief I wrote the vision down and I also saved it electronically. How I did that I do not know as I was not sure that something would come out of it.

I convinced myself that I was not smart enough to write a short story or column let alone a book. At one time as I was cleaning up I came across the note pad I had written the title and deliberately ripped it and dumped it. Now I know that I only dumped the paper, but the vision remained. As I yielded myself to God and started having meaningful fellowship with Him, He began to revive the dreams and visions I had not nurtured, and I also started discovering my purpose as God is revealing it to me. The beginning of the year 2017, the Lord said I should give birth to what I have conceived, and I am glad to say, "This is It".

Thankfully, God Almighty had not written me off even when I had done so to myself. He did not allow my vision to die even though I thought I had aborted it when I ripped the notepad, He was preserving the electronic copy which I thought was lost when our desktop crushed. I did not know anything about cloud storage then although I was using it. I was blessed with a modern computer and as I set up and logged in enjoying God's provision, the title "Rising Above" was right there in One Drive staring at me. I eventually gave in and started working on it slowly and privately with no plans of making it public. I kept it to myself because I did not want anyone to be asking me questions or encourage me to fulfil purpose, despite my efforts to conceal this, The Holy Spirit kept on encouraging me until I was able to mention it, hesitantly though. I would say it in such a way that no one would revisit the subject nor take me seriously. Eventually one morning I forwarded the script to my beloved friend and sister and who is an encourager. I forwarded the script to her, but I was not bold enough to tell her what it was, after a few days she enquired, and I asked her to read it and tell me if it was making any sense at all. We progressed from there. I am grateful to God for bringing her into my life and into my family. When we met I never thought that she was my Elizabeth. Her feedback after going through the script gave me confidence to tell my children that I am writing a book. God bless you sister Effie!

As God inspired me to write this book He was upholding me to Rise Above and Fulfil Purpose. If I could do it, you can do it too by God's grace. As God reveals His purpose for your life, run with the purpose for His grace is sufficient for you. Grace is the energy we need to fulfil purpose.

This is it, my purpose and my testimony of victory in Jesus.

Notes

Notes

Notes

_____

_____

_____

_____

_____

_____

_____

_____

_____

_____

_____

Notes

Made in the USA
Columbia, SC
31 August 2018